*St Briavels Castle*

# THE CASTLES OF
# GLOUCESTERSHIRE
# AND BRISTOL

## Mike Salter

FOLLY PUBLICATIONS

# ACKNOWLEDGEMENTS

Most of the photographs were taken by the author. Other views are reproduced from old postcards in the author's collection. Two views of Berkeley Castle are reproduced by courtesy of Heritage House Group. The author also drew the map and the plans, which are on scales of 1:400, 1:800, 1:2000, and 1:4000, like those in the other castle books in this series. Thanks are due Marjorie Salter for checking proofs, Kate Miles for providing material for some of the plans, and John Cotterill, warden of the youth hostel at St Briavels Castle, who commissioned the guide book to St Briavels produced by Mike in 1998. Thanks also to Helen Thomas, who drove on several field trips and took the photos of the mottes at Lasborough and Newington Bagpath.

## AUTHOR'S NOTES

This series of books (see full list inside back cover) are intended as portable field guides giving as much information and illustrative material as possible in volumes of modest size, weight and price. As a whole the series aims to make information available about less well known buildings. The aim in the castle books has been to mention, where the information is known to the author, owners or custodians of buildings who erected or altered parts of them, and those who were the first or last of a line to hold an estate, an important office, or a title. Those in occupation at the time of dramatic events such as sieges or royal visits are often also named. Other owners and occupants whose lives had little effect on the condition of the buildings are generally not mentioned, nor are ghost stories, myths and legends.

The books are intended to be used in conjunction with the Ordnance Survey 1:50,000 scale maps. Grid references are given in the gazetteer, together with a coded system indicating which sites can be visited or easily seen by the public from adjacent open spaces which is explained on page xx. Generally speaking, maps will be required to find the lesser known sites and earthworks hidden in woods and fields.

Each level of a building is called a storey in this book, the basement being the first storey with its floor near courtyard level unless specifically mentioned as otherwise.

Measurements given in the text and scales on the plans are in metres, the unit used by the author for all measurements taken on site. Although the buildings were designed using feet the metric scales are much easier to use and are now standard amongst academics working on historic buildings and ancient sites. For those who feet a need to make a conversion 3 metres is almost 10 feet. Unless specifically mentioned as otherwise all dimensions are external at or near ground level, but above the plinth if there is one. On the plans the original work is shown black, post 1800 work is stippled and alterations and additions of intermediate periods are hatched.

## ABOUT THE AUTHOR

Mike Salter is 48 and has been a professional writer and publisher since he went on the Government Enterprise Allowance Scheme for unemployed people in 1988. He is particularly interested in the planning and layout of medieval buildings and has a huge collection of plans of castles and churches he has measured during tours (mostly by bicycle and motorcycle) throughout all parts of the British Isles since 1968. Wolverhampton born and bred, Mike now lives in an old cottage beside the Malvern Hills. His other interests include walking, maps, railways, board games, morris dancing, playing percussion instruments and calling dances with a folk group.

Copyright 2002 by Mike Salter. First published March 2002.
Folly Publications, Folly Cottage, 151 West Malvern Rd, Malvern, Worcs, WR14 4AY
Printed by Aspect Design, 89 Newtown Rd, Malvern, Worcs, WR14 2PD

*Thornbury Castle*

## CONTENTS

A map of sites described appears inside the front cover.

# INTRODUCTION

The type of defensible residence known to the Normans as a castle was introduced to England in the mid 11th century. There were Normans in England before Duke William of Normandy's successful invasion of 1066 but it was only then that they took control of the country. Having taken the English Crown William granted estates to his followers in return for periods of military service. The Norman lords or barons then in turn gave units of land called manors to their knights, again in return for military service, this system being called feudalism. The thin veneer of land-owning Normans consolidated their fragile hold on the land by constructing castles serving as residences, strongholds and as symbols of lordly rank. The Romans and Saxons built purely military forts and defences around settlements but the Normans introduced the idea of powerful individuals erecting fortresses to serve as their residences and administrative centres of groups of manors. The Domesday Book survey commissioned by William I in 1086 to record who was holding what land and what it was then considered to be worth mentions the castle at Gloucester, which is assumed to have been built by the king c1068-70. His cousin William Fitz-Osbern, who was created Earl of Hereford in 1067, founded the castle at Berkeley and possibly also that at Bristol. Many of the other castles have no recorded history and in most cases we cannot assign their foundation to a more definate period than the late 11th century or the first two thirds of the 12th century.

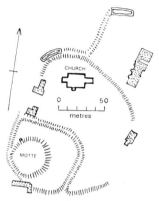

*Plan of English Bicknor Castle*

*Ringwork at Soudley*

*Motte at Castle Tump, Aylesmore, near Dymock*

On a rocky site at Chepstow unsuited to the creation of earthworks William Fitz-Osbern built a stone keep containing a hall over a low basement and two small stone-walled courtyards, but all the early castles in Gloucestershire were not built of mortared stone but of earth and wood. These were quicker and easier materials to work with and in any case there was a comparative lack of stone masons since the Saxons built most of their houses and some of their churches of wood. A common form for early castles was for the lord's house or tower to be raised within a small palisaded court on a high earthen mound or motte surrounded by a ditch. On one side would lie a larger, lower court called a bailey, defended by a rampart with a palisade and ditch, and containing a hall, chapel, workshops, stables, granary, and sundry farm buildings, all timber-framed with roofs of shingles or thatch. The basic design varied according to the terrain and the resources and needs of the builder. An enclosure with a high rampart (now known as a ringwork) was sometimes provided instead of a motte, and baileys were omitted or duplicated and made whatever size and shape local circumstances dictated. Natural landscape features were used where possible, hillocks and spurs being shaped and heightened into steep-sided and level-topped mottes. The Welsh Border counties contain the highest concentration of earthwork castle sites in Britain and there is a fair density of them in the part of Gloucestershire west of the River Severn, an area where ringworks predominate over mottes. Whilst the earthworks at Gloucester and Bristol were probably once quite impressive the other earthwork castle sites in Gloucestershire were mostly on a smaller scale. After nine centuries of erosion they are now generally worn down and in most cases not particularly impressive in their present condition.

Timber is vulnerable to accidental or deliberate destruction by fire and eventually rots away when in contact with damp soil. Although structures of timber remained an important element in the defences of most castles up until the 14th century, the most vital parts would gradually be replaced by walls and towers or mortared stone. Henry I is thought to have erected a stone keep at Gloucester by c1120 and Robert, Earl of Gloucester is assumed to have built that at Bristol in the 1130s. The Giffards built a third large keep at Brimpsfield and two slightly smaller ones lay at Lydney and St Briavels in the Forest of Dean. The general assumption is that these keeps contained three storeys, the lowest level in each case being a storage basement only reached from above, since the entrance was normally placed at second storey level. At Bristol the entrance and the steps up to it were contained in a forebuilding projecting on one side and the Gloucester and Brimpsfield keeps were probably similarly provided. In each case a round-arched entrance doorway would have admitted to a hall with two-light windows in deep round-arched embrasures. In the larger keeps a private room was provided at the same level beyond a crosswall, but the smaller keeps contained only one room at each level, with the lord's private chamber on the topmost storey, above which the walls rose higher to protect the roof. An old sketch shows the Gloucester keep with corner turrets rising up higher, and the Bristol keep was probably also so adorned. In general the appearance and size of these keeps must have been similar to that which survives almost complete except the roof and floors at Rochester in Kent. Nothing now remains visible of any of the Gloucestershire tower keeps, although the lowest parts of those at Lydney and St Briavels have been briefly revealed by excavation, whilst only part of the base revealed by excavation remains of the Bristol keep.

Berkeley has a different type of mid 12th century keep, a shell wall around a court. Usually such shells are built on the tops of mottes but the Berkeley example was built around the motte slopes, thus producing a bigger court within, but necessitating a higher wall than usual. The wall has the usual Norman slender pilaster buttresses and an unusual series of semi-circular bastions, and the entrance and steps up to it are contained in a forebuilding. Although somewhat altered and damaged by a breach made during the Civil War, this keep survives in a fairly complete state.

*The last remains of the gatehouse at Brimpsfield (note portcullis groove)*

*Thornbury Castle*

*Berkeley Castle*

   All the keeps described above were accompanied by stone-walled courtyards built during the second half of the 12th century or the early 13th century, but only at Berkeley and St Briavels does anything significant now remain standing of these walls. St Briavels has a hall-block of 1209-11 comparable to a more ruinous but less altered example at Grosmont in Monmouthshire. Despite much later rebuilding and subdivision the original layout of a hall and chamber over service rooms is still clear. The only other 13th century domestic building to survive is a much altered chamber block at Beverston. This castle, thought to be of the 1220s and 30s, seems to have had a pentagonal court with circular corner towers all of equal size and importance, i.e. there was no keep as such. Although it appears to be an addition or rebuilding of the late 13th century, the gatehouse at Beverston takes a form used at Tamworth, Newcastle and Dover in the early 13th century with two D-shaped towers backed onto a central passageway. St Briavels has a fine twin-towered gatehouse of the 1290s with sophisticated planning and there is a chapel block of c1300. The castle and town walls at Gloucester also had a number of twin-towered gateways of early to mid 13th century date. Only a pair of vaulted porches remain of the splendid 13th royal apartments at Bristol. Very little now remains of the early 14th century castle at Ruardean which probably had a series of circular towers projecting boldly from the corners of a small rectangular court. Berkeley has a fine series of apartments dating from the middle third of the 14th century, when the 12th century outer wall was then mostly rebuilt and provided with a series of buttresses. Only the lower part of a gatehouse remains of an outer court of that period. Apart from rebuilding their main seat the de Berkeleys also remodelled the castle at Beverston, providing rectangular towers in replacement of some the circular original ones. One of the new towers contains a fine vaulted chapel.

*The solar and chapel blocks at St Briavels*

The mid 15th century castle at Sudeley took more the form of an embattled and moated manor house with square inner and outer courts with ranges around all four sides. The inner court had corner towers of varying sizes. Although it was fortified during the Civil War this building was never of much military strength and its defensibility was decreased when Richard, Duke of Gloucester (later Richard III) rebuilt the east range with huge oriel windows facing the field. A final building of this type was built by the Duke of Buckingham as late as 1511-21 at Thornbury. The corner towers and towers flanking the inner gatehouse are polygonal. The one tower completed to full height has a machicolated parapet, the inner and outer gateways have portcullis grooves and there are gunports around the inner entrance but these military features are essentially for show. The large outer court provided extensive lodgings for retainers, in effect a private barracks.

Scattered across Gloucestershire are platforms surrounded by moats which mark the sites of former medieval manor houses, most of which were not otherwise fortified. In many cases the original internal buildings were of perishable materials. Most of the moats date from the 13th and 14th centuries, the most common form being a water-filled ditch about 10m wide and up to 3m deep (but often with barely a metre depth of water) surrounding a roughly rectangular platform from 40m to 60m long. Few Gloucestershire moats have been excavated or properly surveyed so details about their history and true purpose in many cases can only be surmised. The digging of ditches was not regulated by the crown like the construction of embattled walls were from the end of the 12th century onwards, but as only the gentry and wealthier clerics possessed the land and could afford the labour needed to create them, moats were status symbols. They were not necessarily defensive in a military sense. They would serve to keep out vagrants and wild animals and keep in the children, servants and domestic animals of a household. They have always been valued as scenic features and formed a habitat for fish, eels and water fowl, which together formed a substantial part of the diet of the landed classes.

In the medieval period castle walls of rubble were sometimes lime-washed both inside and out, making them look very different to the way they appear today. Dressed stones around windows and doorways would be left uncovered. Domestic rooms would have had murals of biblical, historical or heroic scenes mostly painted in red, yellow and black. Wall hangings decorated with the same themes or heraldry gradually became more common from the 14th century onwards. Although used in churches and chapels (as in Bristol castle chapel in 1245), glass was expensive and uncommon in secular buildings before the 15th century, so windows were originally closed with wooden shutters. As a result rooms were dark when the weather was too cold or wet for them to be opened for light and ventilation. Large openings in the outer walls sometimes had bars or projecting grilles even if high above ground level. Living rooms usually had fireplaces although large halls such as that at Bristol had central hearths with the smoke escaping through louvres in the roof. Small latrine chambers squeezed into the thickness of the outer walls were common.

Furnishings were sparse up until the 15th century, although the embrasures of upper storey windows sometimes have built-in stone seats, as at St Briavels. Lords with several castles tended to circulate around them administering their manorial courts and consuming agricultural produce on the spot. The seats of great lords could be left almost empty when neither they nor their families were in residence. Castles required continual maintenance to keep them either comfortable or defensible and from the late 13th century onwards inventories and surveys of the castles reveal many deficiencies. For much of their lives castles gradually crumbled away with only a skeleton staff to administer the estates. The royal castles of Bristol, Gloucester and St Briavels eventually all became ruinous at the end of the medieval period, except for one or two buildings maintained for the holding of courts and the keeping of prisoners. Servants travelled with their lords and sometimes also portable furnishings such as rugs, wall hangings, cooking vessels and bedding, all kept in wooden chests. The lord and his immediate family and honoured guests and senior household officials would enjoy a fair degree of privacy by the late 13th century, having their own rooms. Servants and retainers enjoyed less comfort and privacy, sharing of beds and communal sleeping in any spaces that were warm being common.

Berkeley (which is open to the public during the summer months) remains the best preserved castle in Gloucestershire, having continuously remained inhabited, despite the damage done to it during the Civil War. During that period the castles of Bristol and Gloucester were totally destroyed. After being abandoned for two centuries the incomplete castle at Thornbury was partly restored and occupied in the 18th century, whilst St Briavels and Sudeley (which are both open to the public) have been partly restored to habitation in more recent times. Part of Beverston also remains habitable. Brimpsfield was destroyed in the early 14th century and it is likely that by then all the earthwork sites never developed in stone had been abandoned.

# PUBLIC ACCESS TO SITES

E   Buildings in the care of English Heritage.
  ·   Access at certain times.
F   Ruins or earthworks to which there is free
      access at any reasonable time.
O   Buildings opened to the public by private
      owners, local councils, trusts, etc.
V   Buildings closely visible from public open
      spaces, roads, paths, or churchyards.

*St Briavels Castle*

# GAZETTEER OF GLOUCESTERSHIRE CASTLES

## BERKELEY CASTLE    ST 685990    O

William Fitz-Osbern, Earl of Hereford founded a castle here in 1067, as recorded in Domesday Book. It may have been damaged or destroyed as a result of Robert Mowbray's rebellion in 1086 but had been rebuilt by 1121 when the second of three successive Roger de Berkeleys entertained Henry I at the castle over Easter. Roger III supported King Stephen and on the latter's death in 1154 Henry II confiscated Berkeley and gave it to the Bristol merchant Robert Fitz-Harding. The king agreed to fortify the castle according to Robert's will and the keep is assumed to be the result of this. A forebuilding to the keep and the inner bailey curtain wall were erected by Robert's son Maurice, who secured his possession by marrying the heiress of Roger de Berkeley III. His son Robert lost the castle for opposing King John, but it was restored to his brother Thomas by Henry III in 1223. His grandson Thomas, who was ransomed after being captured by the Scots at Bannockburn in 1314, was the first of the family to be summoned to Parliament under the title Lord Berkeley. His son Maurice II died a prisoner in Wallingford Castle, having raided the estates of Edward II's unpopular favourite Hugh le Despenser. Thomas, 3rd Lord Berkeley was married to a daughter of Roger Mortimer, who became Earl of March and ruler of the kingdom after he deposed the unpopular Edward II in 1326. The deposed king was eventually imprisoned within the keep at Berkeley and was murdered there in 1327.

*Outer gateway arch at Berkeley*

*The inner gatehouse and keep at Berkeley Castle*

After the fall from power and execution of Roger Mortimer in 1330, when the teenage Edward III began to rule in person, Thomas, 3rd Lord Berkeley managed to remain in favour with the young king, serving him abroad as a diplomat. During this period the hall and apartments were remodelled in a lavish new style. The inner and outer gatehouses are also of this period and it can be assumed that the work also included the construction of the wall of the outer ward, now destroyed down to courtyard level. On the death of Thomas, 5th Lord Berkeley in 1417 the castle passed to his nephew James, (whose effigy lies in the church) for whom the title was created anew by Henry VI, although there was a dispute over his possession of the castle. His son William surrendered the castle to Henry VII in exchange for the extra titles of Marquis of Berkeley and Earl of Nottingham. These honours died with him in 1491 and the castle remained in royal hands until restored to George, Lord Berkeley in 1553 at the accession of Queen Mary. He carried out some remodelling to the apartments and was succeeded in 1613 by his son, another George.

In 1645 a Royalist garrison surrendered the castle to a Parliamentary force after a three day siege. The apartments seem to have been left intact but a section of the outer wall of the keep was destroyed down to the level of the motte top, either as a form of slighting afterwards, or possibly by bombardment during the conflict. The curtain wall of the outer court was also breached or entirely removed at this time.

In 1676 the third George, Lord Berkeley was created an earl by Charles II. After the death of Frederick Augustus, 5th Earl of Berkeley, in 1810, the title was disputed between his elder sons, who were considered illegitimate, and his younger sons born after his marriage. In the end the title went to a younger son but the castle went to the eldest son, William, created Lord Fitz-Hardinge by Queen Victoria in 1841. The 8th Earl of Berkeley, a descendant of Sir George Berkeley, a younger brother of Frederick Augustus, regained the castle in 1916 on the death of Charles, 3rd Lord FitzHardinge, but both titles died with him in 1942. More recently the castle has been occupied by descendants of Sir James Berkeley, younger brother of the William who died in 1491.

*Plan of Berkeley Castle*

*Berkeley Castle*

*Berkeley Castle*

Berkeley Castle consisted of a motte with an inner bailey 55m across south of it and an outer bailey of similar size to the west. The ground falls away on the SW and SE sides but rises slightly towards the churchyard on the north, from which the site is separated by a ditch which may once have been water filled. Of the outer bailey walls and buildings only the lower stage of the gatehouse remains. It is a rectangular 14th century structure and the destroyed curtain wall was probably also of that period. The outer archway is finely moulded and has a portcullis groove.

The keep of c1154-6 is an unusual type of shell keep which encases the motte rather than stands upon its summit, thus producing a wall which is 14m high on the outside but only 9m high on the inside. The wall is embattled, buttressed at intervals and was flanked by four semi-circular turrets 6m in diameter which are the same height as the wall. The turrets were added after the wall was built to motte summit-height, and the two were then continued up as one build. One of them has been replaced by the Thorpe Tower on the north side and another is mostly enveloped by the inner gatehouse. Another, facing east, contains the vaulted apse of the chapel of St John above two lower levels, the inner part being a modern rebuild. The Thorpe Tower is a 17m long and 15m high length of 5m thick walling from which project two turrets. It contains a spiral stair and looks as if it might have once been a massive square tower, the outer part of which has been destroyed. The keep is entered by means of steps within a forebuilding on the east side rising to a Norman doorway into which a narrower later doorway has been inserted. The court inside contains apartments on the south and SE. On the west is the breach made in the shell wall in the 1640s. In the 1920s the puzzling feature of the lower part of a row of stone columns was discovered running across the middle of the court.

The rectangular inner gateway lies SW of the keep and contains two storeys of rooms over a passage closed by a portcullis at its inner end and flanked to the SW by a guard-room. Close to the keep the upper levels have cross-shaped arrow-loops and towards the court the third storey is supported on modern corbelling. The inner ward is crammed with apartments all the way round from the gatehouse to where there is a narrow northward facing postern beside the keep forebuilding. Although of 12th century origin the outer wall is heavily buttressed and in places pierced by windows so much of it is now 14th century work and later. On the SE is the hall, which is 18.5m long by 9.5m wide and has four closely spaced windows facing the court between a vaulted porch opening onto the screens passage at the NE end and a stair projection at the other end, entered under a "Berkeley arch" - a cinquefoiled arch with cusped ogees. A Victorian porch has been added in front of the latter. The hall is essentially 14th century, like most of the domestic buildings, but traces of round-headed Norman windows are visible in the hall outer wall. Two of these now contain French medieval windows inserted in the 1920s, when the fireplace at the SW end was also brought in. Off the screens passage open cinquefoil-headed doorways to a pantry and buttery with a passage between them to a hexagonal kitchen 6m across with three fireplaces and an original roof. The bakehouse beyond is spanned by a pair of flat stone arches. The NE range was remodelled in the 16th century and again in the 1920s.

The private apartments lie along the SW side, beginning with a triangular vaulted cellar next to the hall. It formed a lobby to a much altered lower suite of rooms for officials. Over the cellar is the Morning Room, created in 1923 from the 14th century chapel of St Mary. It has ogival arches towards a narrow passageway on the south side. It has an original roof painted in red and green with verses of the revelation of St John translated into English by John Trevisa, one of the castle chaplains. The Long Drawing Room was originally the lord's private hall and his bedroom beyond was originally reached only via a small polygonal turret facing the court. The rooms at the end of the range, next to the gatehouse, were added in the 15th century. The bedrooms throughout the south range have 15th and 16th century fireplaces and various modifications of the 1920s.

*Beverston   Castle*

*Gateway tower at Beverston*

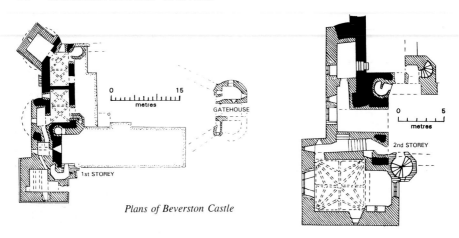

*Plans of Beverston Castle*

# BEVERSTON CASTLE    ST 892940    V

In 1229 Henry III granted a licence for a castle which Maurice de Gaunt had recently erected. The full original shape of the court is not known but the present house on the south side containing mullion-and-transom windows of c1700 stands on the site of a hall which seems to have had arcades sides, and private chambers were contained in a three storey block on the west side of the court. The lowest level of this range, which is 7.5m wide externally, contains two rooms each rib-vaulted in two bays. Above were two levels of rooms 14m long by not much more than 4m wide, both with 16th century fireplaces. Projecting from the SW and NW corners of this block were round towers. The gatehouse probably dates from the end of the 13th century, although its plan form of two D-shaped towers 7m in diameter containing guard rooms with their straight sides backing onto a passage closed by a portcullis at the inner end resembles gatehouses of Henry III's reign at Tamworth and Dover. There was just a single large room above. This gatehouse begs the question of what form of gatehouse was originally provided in the 1220s. Was it, for instance, no more than a barbican gateway in front of an older inner gateway, in which case the original castle would have been about 28m square externally.

Between 1330 and 1361 the castle was remodelled by Thomas, Lord Berkeley. The southern of the two round towers was shaved off to become part of a projection connecting the private chambers with a new SW corner tower 10.5m by 9m. The lowest level has a rib vault. The chapel above is a remarkable room with a square nave covered by a tierceron vault with bosses and a small east chancel with its own rib-vault, a three light east window, a corner piscina and a pair of sedilia with crocketted ogival arches. Passages linked this chapel to the west end of the hall and the old solar beyond. Above was the lord's chamber, this room and another further north both having squints in towards a tiny second chapel squeezed in between them. This chapel or oratory also has a piscina and the remains of a circular window looking out over the hall roof. The spiral stair in a turret on the NE corner of this tower is 16th century. In the 15th century the NW round tower was replaced by a rectangular tower 7.5m by 6.5m set diagonally. Above a basement with a single loop it contains two bedrooms, now both derelict, with latrines in the south corner. A spiral stair linked these rooms and the upper one had direct access from a spiral stair in a polygonal turret of the same period provided at the NE corner of the chamber block. Another stair turret lies at the SE corner of the block, adjacent to the hall.

The Berkeley family sold the castle in 1597 and in 1612 it went to Sir Michael Hicks, who probably built the present south range. The castle was captured by Parliamentary forces after two sieges in 1644 and was probably then partly dismantled. It was re-roofed after a fire in 1691. As seen from the east, where there are two old barns, one of them 14th century, the castle looks quite at home in the Cotswolds but the west aspect, with two rectangular towers, one diagonally set, rising out of a dry ditch, reminds one of castles in the north of England.

## BRIMPSFIELD CASTLE    SO 942127

After John Giffard was executed in 1322 for his part in the rebellion of Thomas, Earl of Lancaster, Edward II ordered that his castle of Brimpsfield was to be destroyed and the manor given to the king's favourite Hugh le Despencer. Inquistions of 1327 and 1338 describe the castle as ruinous and there is no evidence the site was ever reoccupied. By 1338 the manor had passed to the Berkeleys. It later went to the Mortimers and then back to the Crown. All that remains of the castle is a partly stone-revetted moat up to 30m wide around an oval space 120m by 95m which was divided into two courts, the inner of which, at least, had a stone curtain wall with four towers. Excavations in 1920 and 1936 revealed part of the base of a SW facing gatehouse. The portcullis groove is still visible but there is no sign of the staircase to the upper storeys mentioned by the excavators. A central depression is thought to be the site of a rectangular keep 18m by 20s with a forebuilding on the east side.

The 3m high motte lying above a stream 0.5km to the east at 946127 may have been erected by Osbern Giffard, who was given the manor c1086. The stone castle is thought to have replaced it during the 1140s and became the Giffards' chief seat. King John seized the castle in 1215 after Helias Giffard and his brother Osbert rebelled against him, but Helias regained his lands from Henry III in 1217.

## BLEDISLOE MOTTE    SO 683082

In the 1970s a motte SW of Bledisloe Farm was removed after an excavation.

*Beverston: gateway portcullis groove*

*Beverston Castle*

## BRISTOL CASTLE   592731   F

A few fragments of this once mighty fortress lie in a park above the north bank of the Avon. The remains include the base of the northern half of a tower keep, a sallyport or postern, a length of the south curtain wall with two loopholes of cellars beside the river, and two rib-vaulted 13th century porches, now almost disguised externally by modern work. The southern porch led into the south or service end of an aisled great hall seven bays long, measuring about 32m by 16m, which was built by Henry III in 1239-42, whilst the northern porch was added c1300 to give access to the royal apartments lying on the west side of the hall. A pantry and buttery lay south of the hall, and a kitchen lay against the curtain wall east of them. The keep was a cube of about 24m over walls up to 4.5m thick and was divided by a cross-wall. It had four corner turrets, one higher than the rest, and a forebuilding on the east side, where a well-shaft remains in the walling of the main building. A latrine pit survives on the west side. It is likely that the keep contained three storeys, with a gallery around the topmost level, and with the walls rising high above the roofs. The sallyport adjoined the constable's house which lay by the main gatehouse in the SW corner.

The castle may have been founded c1068 by William Fitz-Osbern, Earl of Hereford. It is first mentioned in 1088 when Geoffrey, Bishop of Coutances and Robert Mowbray were using it as a rebel base against William II and it is possible that the castle was then newly built by the bishop. The keep was built by Robert, Earl of Gloucester, being completed by 1141, when King Stephen was held within it after being captured at Lincoln. The keep seems to have replaced a large motte. Henry II took over the castle after the rebellion in 1173-4 and since he spent very little on it we can be fairly sure that it was already well provided with stone walls and buildings.

Henry III was responsible for much work on the castle and had his cousin Eleanor of Brittany kept prisoner within it from 1224 until her death in 1241. The L-shaped barbican built in front of the west gate in 1220 crossed the ditch and then turned north, although its outer portal seems to have faced west. Construction of the hall was followed by that of a new gateway, and in 1245 the windows in the king's chapel were glazed. In 1276 Edward I, who had possessed the castle since being given it upon his marriage to Eleanor of Castile in 1254, had work done on the main chapel and the private apartments under the supervision of William of Mountsorrell. Collapsed sections of the south curtain wall were rebuilt in 1288 abd 1294-5.

*South curtain wall at Bristol*

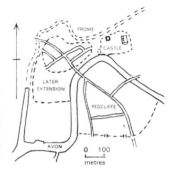

*Plan of Bristol town walls*

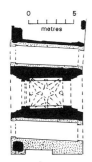

*Bristol: town gateway*

*The base of the keep at Bristol*

In 1312 the castle was under the control of Bartholomew de Badlesmere, who so antagonised the townsfolk that they placed the castle under a sort of state of siege by refusing supplies and building a barrier between it and the town. To sort out this situation Edward was forced to send a force led by Earl of Pembroke and a naval force under Lord Berkeley. Edward II was kept prisoner at the castle in 1326 prior to his incarceration and eventual murder at Berkeley in 1327. In later years the castle was held in dower by various queen consorts. It was repaired by Henry VI in 1441 and 1447 and Edward IV had further work done in 1464-6. It subsequently decayed and the great hall was in ruins by the 1480s. The castle did not play a significant part in the Civil War but was nonetheless demolished by order of Parliament in 1655.

Bristol was one of England's most important towns throughout the medieval period. By the 12th century an oval area about 500m by 300m defined by Bristol Bridge, Baldwin St, St Stephen St, Nelson St and Fairfax St had been enclosed with a stone wall. The castle guarded the east end of the town, which was otherwise enclosed by the Avon and the Frome. The church of St John the Baptist adjoins the 15th century North Gate, with its tower and spire standing over the gateway passage, which is fan-vaulted and has a portcullis groove, whilst the church has a crypt built against the town wall. The church of St Nicholas also lies over a medieval crypt built against a (hidden) section of the town wall. The adjacent South Gate was destroyed in 1762, prior to a new church being built over the crypt.

By the 13th century the River Frome (now mostly culverted), which ran along the north and west sides of the Norman town, had been diverted to allow an expansion of the town to the SW onto a marshy promontory at the confluence of the rivers. In the 1260s the point of the promontory was cut off by a new wall with two gates and several D-shaped towers, the base of one of which still remains (although hidden), having been excavated in 1970. A still larger extension, more than doubling the walled area was the enclosing of the suburb of Redcliffe south of the river between 1239 and 1247, although the church of St Mary Redcliffe lay outside the walls.

## CIRENCESTER CASTLE

A castle built in 1142 was captured by King Stephen later the same year. Its location is not known. The Roman town defences may have survived into the medieval period although the only remnants now are parts of the rampart NW of London Road and in Watermoor Gardens at the SE corner. A rampart and ditch strengthened with stone turrets and gatehouses enclosed an area of 240 acres. Part of the large gateway on the NE has been excavated. In the early 3rd century the rampart was given a stone outer wall to which polygonal bastions were added in the late 4th century.

# DIXTON CASTLE   SO 986305

The whole top of an isolated hill 4km NW of Winchcombe is defended by earthworks. The outer ward may be an adaptation of an Iron Age fort but there is a motte towards the east end with a bailey beyond it. The manor was held by the Dixton family in the 12th century as tenants of the earls of Gloucester, but in 1166 Roger Dixton headed a list of the tenants of Winchcombe Abbey. Dixton passed to the Higfords in 1413.

# DURSLEY CASTLE

The site of the castle held by supporters of the Empress Matilda against King Stephen in the 1140s is uncertain. It became the chief seat of the de Berkeley family for a short period after Henry II took Berkeley Castle from them in 1154.

# DYMOCK CASTLE   SO 713294

The motte and bailey at Castle Tump, Aylesmore are thought to represent the castle of "Dimoc" which existed during Stephen's reign.

# ENGLISH BICKNOR CASTLE   SO 581157

The church lies in an outer bailey to the north of a bailey about 60m across containing a motte on the SW side with a summit 30m across, upon which a chamber 3.6m square was discovered in 1875. There is a well below the mound NW side. In the 13th century the manor was held by the Muchegros family. See page 4.

# GLOUCESTER CASTLE   SO 832183

The castle is mentioned in Domesday Book in 1086 as having taken space formerly occupied by 16 houses, and is assumed to have been founded by William I. Since the Evesham survey of 1097 mentions 24 houses having been destroyed it is likely that William II added an outer bailey. The original rectangular bailey 110m by 90m lay within the west corner of the Roman city defences, with a motte occupying its north corner. Traces of a building in the bailey have been located in Ladybellegate St. Excavations in 1990 found evidence that the motte proved to be unstable because of movement of sand below it, and Henry I replaced it by a large tower keep, located further NW beyond the Roman walls. This tower is first mentioned in 1112 and is shown in a 14th century sketch as being of three storeys with corner turrets rising above it. A curtain wall was eventually built around a bailey 130m across surrounding this keep. Henry II had the walls repaired in the 1180s, when a tower over the gateway is mentioned. The original bailey was abandoned and the SE part of it later became part of the precinct of the Dominican friary, which existed by 1239, Henry III being a principal benefactor. Some sort of barbican seems to have been erected over the site of the motte, although the main gateway of the new stone castle faced NE, and a barbican added by Henry III faced towards a new bridge over the river.

When Prince John was given the honour of Gloucester in 1189 on his marriage to Isabel, daughter of William, 3rd Earl of Gloucester, the castle of Gloucester was kept in royal hands. Nevertheless it seems to have been taken over by Prince John at some point since the regent William Longchamp besieged it when John rebelled in 1193. The castle was captured in 1263 by supporters of Simon de Montfort, after a short-lived attempt by some of the garrison to hold out in the keep after the bailey had fallen. A force of Marcher lords attempted to retake the castle for Henry III in 1264 and it was eventually recaptured by Prince Edward in 1265. The castle was maintained by the Crown until the late 15th century but then fell into ruin.

The Roman town rampart was fronted by a stone wall and enclosed an area 500m by 400m with round corners with square internal towers facing the cardinal points. The Roman road layout of a crossing of two main roads with gates near the middle of each side still remains. The Roman defences seem to have mostly survived into the medieval period, the city having held out against a Danish attack in 914. However, the Norman abbey church (now the cathedral) lies over the site of the north corner, so the medieval defences took a sweep to the north at that point and continued further west to enclose the new suburb between the West Gate and the River Severn. The site of East Gate in the middle of the SE side of the Roman town is marked on the ground. The Roman gateway there had rectangular guard rooms flanking the passage. It was rebuilt as an inward projecting square tower in the 11th century and then in the mid 13th century two round towers were added, the north one projecting out further towards the field than its twin. This tower served as the female prison in 1584. The gatehouse was later used as a workhouse until demolition in 1778.

When the Civil War broke out in 1642 but the castle and city walls were in a very ruinous condition, part of the NE wall of the city having fallen the previous year. An earth rampart was then built inside the wall round from the North Gate to the South Gate, the ditch cleared out and houses demolished to allow the defenders a clear field of fire. At some point the line of the city defences was extended to the NE, making a hexagonal layout with a short NE side. Polygonal earth bastions were later erected, as shown on a plan of 1780 (probably based on a plan of the 1640s showing what it was intended to build), and an outwork on the west side of the Severn. Excavations have revealed traces of the ditch in front of a bastion 90m wide built in front of the South Gate, and of a ditch dug within East Gate by the defenders in September 1643, towards the end of an unsuccessful siege by Charles I lasting a month. Work on the fortifications continued in 1644, and further works were executed in 1650-1, but in 1653 several of the bastions were dismantled and the soil transferred to parts of the west side of the city subject to flooding. What remained of the defences of both the city and castle were demolished in 1662 by order of Charles II, because of the city's strong support of Parliament in the war. The prison of the 1790s stands on the site of the castle.

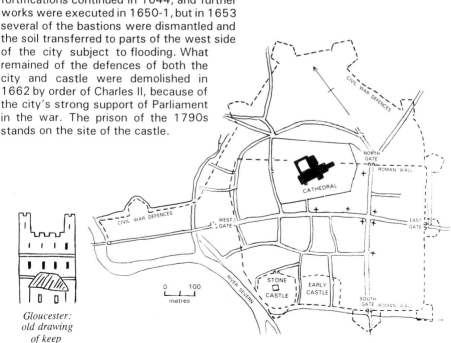

*Gloucester: old drawing of keep*

*Plan of Gloucester city defences*

*The ringwork at Littledean*

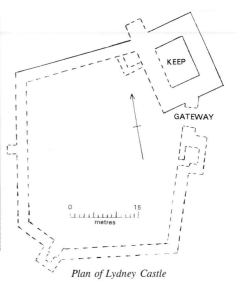

KEEP

GATEWAY

0                15
metres

*Plan of Lydney Castle*

# HAILES CASTLE    SP 056301    F

The earthworks buried in Hailes Wood 0.5km east of the church may be the site of the castle that existed in the 1140s. Closer to the church are traces of a later moat.

# HARESFIELD CASTLE    SO 810105    V

Beyond the north side of the churchyard is The Mount, an overgrown moated platform 3m high and 40m across on top.

# HASFIELD COURT    SO 825274    V

Hasfield was held by the Pauncefoote family from 1200 until they sold the property in 1598, having been fined as Catholic recusants. The house was remodelled in the 1860s but retains some early 16th and late 17th century features. South of it is a deep and wide ditch, whilst in the stable block to the NW, close to the road, is an archway of c1500 flanked by quatrefoil openings, from the former outer gatehouse.

# HEWELSFIELD MOTTE    SO 568021

Behind buildings SE of the church are slight traces of a motte.

# LASBOROUGH MOTTE    ST 824941    V

This is a damaged or incomplete motte on flat land above a slope into a valley.

# LITTLEDEAN RINGWORK    SO 677136    F

On the end of a ridge commanding wide views over the Severn estuary is a ringwork 33m across and rising up to 5m above the 2m deep ditch. This is probably the Old Castle of Dean mentioned in a mid 12th century document. The bank contains a lot of stone and may represent the buried stump of a curtain wall, although the none was recorded when the bank was sectioned in an excavation many years ago.

*Lasborough Motte*

## LYDNEY CASTLE   SO 617024

On a bluff in Lydney Park 0.5km north of Aylburton Church lie the half-buried footings of a small castle, excavated in 1930. The finds included pottery, buckles, keys, nails, shears, a padlock bolt, a boathook and a pick. A wall between 2m and 3m thick surrounded a quadrangular court 36m by 32m with the SW corner cut off by a wall from which projected a turret. The base of a tower keep 17m by 14m over walls 3m thick remains at the NE corner. It had a turret projecting from the NW corner and an internal building was later built between the keep and the curtain here. Between the keep and a tower 9m by 5.5m in the middle of the east side was the gateway. From it came a stone with a double roll-moulding found in the excavation.

## MISERDEN CASTLE   SO 944093

A motte and bailey lie in trees on a strong promontory site above the west bank of the River Frome. The bailey protects the landward side of the motte, which has traces of a shell wall. This must have been the castle which was surrendered to King Stephen's forces after they captured Robert Musard and threatened to hang him. In 1230 a later Robert Musard broke into the castle during a family quarrel. The castle was seized by the sheriff of Gloucester and then returned to its owner Ralph Musard, who was rebuked for not keeping an adequate guard within it. The castle was still in use in the 1260s but seems to have been abandoned by 1289.

## NEWINGTON BAGPATH MOTTE   ST 817948

0     15
metres

*Newington Bagpath*

This motte lies high above the west side of a tributary of the Little Avon River, the site being less than a kilometre from the motte at Lasborough. The motte rises 3m above the ditch on its west and south sides to a dished summit 25m by 18m.

*Newington Bagpath Motte*

*Newnham-on-Severn Castle*

# NEWNHAM-ON-SEVERN CASTLE    SO 817948    F

The church lies above a cliff to the River Severn and west of it are earthworks of what in a charter of c1240 was described as the site of an old castle. Newnham was made a borough in 1187 and for a long time was the only one in Gloucestershire west of the Severn. There is no evidence that it was fortified in the medieval period and the rampart extending northwards from the castle site probably dates from a military occupation in 1643, when the castle site was probably put back into use.

*Rampart at Newnham-on-Severn*

*Ruardean Castle*

# RUARDEAN CASTLE   SO 619180

On a ridge NW of the church are traces of two enclosures and a fragment of the lower part of a boldly projecting circular corner tower 8m in diameter, the octagonal basement room of which had a rib-vault. In 1311 Edward II licensed Alexander de Bykenore, Treasurer of Ireland, to crenellate the building. It passed to Richard de Karent and then to the Walwyn family.

*Ruardean Castle: plan*

*Ruardean Castle*

## ST BRIAVELS CASTLE   SO 558045   E

William I gave the Forest of Dean to William Fitz-Osbern, Earl of Hereford but there is nothing to suggest that the latter built anything at St Briavels. After the rebellion in 1075 of his son Roger de Breteuil the forest became a crown possession again under a royal bailiff. The bailiffs needed an administrative centre and the castle is most likely to have been built to serve that function during Henry I's reign. The probability is that it was erected when Walter Durand was Sheriff of Gloucester. It is first mentioned in Henry I's Pipe Rolls for 1129-30 when Walter's son Miles of Gloucester spent £13 5s 7d on providing a knight, porter and watch. After King Stephen was defeated by Henry I's daughter Matilda at Lincoln in 1141 she confirmed Miles in possession of St Briavels and created him Earl of Hereford. In 1155 Matilda's son Henry II, who had recently succeeded Stephen as king, recovered the castle and the Forest of Dean from Miles' son Roger after a short confrontation. The castle then remained with the crown under a series of bailiffs. It is likely that Henry II stayed at the castle when he came to hunt in the Forest of Dean in 1158.

There are records of the manufacture of axes, picks, shovels, nails and horseshoes in the district in the late 12th century and the dispatch of these iron products for royal military campaigns in Ireland and the Holy Land. It is assumed that these munitions were stored at the castle prior to dispatch but the royal records make no specific mention of either the castle or the administration of the forest between a royal visit in 1164 and a mention of repairs to the castle in 1195. It is assumed that the stone tower keep which once stood on the south side was built during this period, and perhaps also the curtain wall.

King John spent £5 on maintenance of the castle in 1202 and visited it in February 1205 and November 1207, when he was visited by the Welsh lord Cruffydd ap Cadwallon. John was probably again in residence in the castle in March 1209 when the town was granted the right to hold a weekly market. Hugh Neville, chief forester of the Forest of Dean spent £291 12s 6d upon building works at St Briavels between 1209 and 1211, and to this period can be assigned the hall block which would have provided King John with improved accommodation for his visits during the autumns of 1212 and 1213.

*West side of St Briavels Castle*

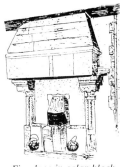

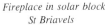

*Fireplace in solar block St Briavels*

*Curtain wall at St Briavels*

There are many references to the castle during Henry III's long reign (1216-72). The then bailiff, Roger Clifford, had the keep and other buildings repaired in 1224, and the king stayed at St Briavels in 1226 and 1228. In the latter year John Malemort and his brother William the Smith and William the Fletcher were sent to the castle to produce quarrels (crossbow-bolts) there. By 1233 they were producing 12,000 quarrels in a 120 day period and in 1237 there is a record of 20,000 quarrels being sent to the Constable of Dover. In 1234 the castle was garrisoned against a revolt by Richard Marshall. There is no record of an attack on the castle by the rebels but it was much repaired in the years immediately afterwards. The ditch was cleared out, a new drawbridge provided, a timber chapel erected before the doorway to the king's chamber, and the masonry of the keep repaired. In 1247 a new chamber was erected for the king's knights. The keep and drawbridge were repaired in 1249-50 and in 1255 a section of recently fallen curtain wall was rebuilt. The sheriff of Gloucester spent £76 in 1260 on repairing the farm buildings outside the castle (probably to the west of it), plastering the interior of the middle storey of the keep, and rebuilding the barricades and barbican in front of the entrance gateway with timber from the forest.

In 1277 Edward I ordered 200,000 quarrels to be sent from St Briavels for his campaign in North Wales and another 170,000 were ordered for a second campaign in 1283. A new twin-towered gatehouse was erected on the north side between May 1292 and November 1293, the custodian John Botetourt spending over £415 on works using local stone and timber, plus £63 on lead for the gatehouse roof. Between 1307 and 1312 custodian John Handlo spent almost £323 on repairing the towers, bridges and buildings, plus the construction of a peel or palisaded area on the south side. In 1312 £11 was spent on fixing 61 wooden "targes" upon the walls in expectation of an attack after the murder of the king's favourite Piers Gaveston. Despite further repairs in 1318 the peel was described as ruinous in 1323 and in 1325-6 it was replaced by a stone wall costing £40. At the same time repairs were carried out on the new gatehouse, the round tower, the hall, pantry buttery, kitchen, king's chamber, chapel, wardrobe, knight's chamber, stable and bakehouse, and the roof of the keep. When Edward II was deposed in 1326 the castle was handed over to his wife Isabella but after her lover Roger Mortimer was executed by the young Edward III in 1330 the castle was taken back by the crown. Over £200 was spent on repairs to the hall, gatehouse, drawbridge and a tower on the east side between 1331 and 1335, and small sums continued to be spent on it from time to time, plus the larger sum of £108 in 1363. Richard II granted St Briavels to his uncle Thomas, Duke of Gloucester but recovered it after Thomas was arrested at Calais in 1397.

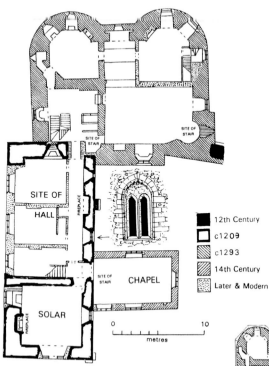

*St Briavels: plan of upper storey*

By the 15th century the castle ceased to be used for the manufacture and storage of munitions, and the occasional royal visited ceased also. It was generally neglected, although repairs to the gatehouse and drawbridge are recorded in the 1470s, when Edward IV's consort Elizabeth Woodville held the constableship. The decayed castle continued to be used for courts for the administration of the Forest of Dean. The Free Miners were allowed to enact laws enforced at their own private courts held in the castle (and occasionally elsewhere) until 1754.

By the 16th century the courts of the Free Miners were held in the castle chapel with the solar serving as a jury retiring room. The hall seems to have then been ruinous, Camden describing the castle in the 1580s as half demolished. By 1692 the only parts not ruinous were the chapel, solar and the western half of the gatehouse, which served as a prison. From 1850 until 1910 rooms in the castle served as a parochial school. It then became a private residence, the hall block being rebuilt and new windows inserted in the other parts. Now maintained by English Heritage, the building has been leased by the crown to the Youth Hostels Association since 1947, who hold medieval banquets in the dining room in the chapel block.

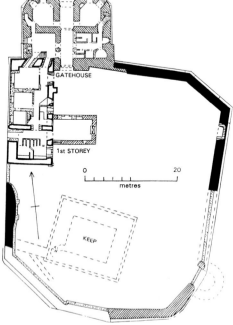

*Plan of St Briavels Castle*

The castle consists of a court measuring 50m from north to south by 43m wide situated on a spur rising 200m above the River Wye. The court has remains of a 12th century curtain wall 2m thick above a sloping plinth. Around the NE corner wall is 6m high above the interior. The moat was drained in the 1850s and has been filled in on the west side. The ground at the south end of the court is now 3m higher than the court between the gatehouse and chapel. Just north of the SE corner is a length of thin modern walling closing off a gap where a tower about 8m across once lay. In the original late 12th century layout there was a gatehouse close to here, which was commanded by the adjacent keep in the middle of the south side, and the 14th century walling here represents an extension to enclose what was originally a barbican on this side. The upper parts of the keep fell in 1752 and all that now remains visible of it are three fallen chunks of core-masonry. Excavations in 1970-2 revealed the lower part of the SW corner with the lowest steps of a spiral stair and also located the northern corners (the SE corner lies under a tree) showing it to be 15.6m long by 13.9m wide with walls 3m thick above the plinth. Fragments of a round chimney with quatrefoil holes in the side found near the NE corner probably dated from King John's reign, although the keep may have been built as early as Henry I's reign, since there is no mention of expenditure by Henry II on such a major building project. It is probable that there were two upper rooms forming a living room or hall and private chamber over a dark storage basement.

The domestic block of 1209-11 has replaced the northern half of the west curtain wall. This block is 22.2m long by 9.9m wide, the east and south walls being 1.4m thick, whilst the other walls, which faced the field, were up to 2.3m thick. On the upper storey the block originally contained a hall 12.3m long by 6.6m wide at the north end (now divided into two dormitories, an office and a passage) and an almost square solar at the south end which is used as the youth hostel common room. A doorway with a pointed arch of two orders now facing into the chapel block formed the hall entrance and probably gave onto a passage divided off from the hall proper by a screen. The dais for the lord's table was at the north end and the dormitory there contains a segmental arched embrasure containing seats set high above the floor level and having a later 13th century trefoil-headed window later blocked by the addition of the gatehouse. The northern window in the passage may also be late 13th century but the larger window with twin lancets further south is original early 13th century work. It is likely that there were once two or three similar windows in the west wall, which in modern times has mostly been rebuilt much thinner at both levels. The solar has an original east window, an altered west window with seats in the embrasure, and a crudely reassembled fireplace, possibly from the east wall of the hall, where there is a recess onto which backs a much rebuilt buttress. The solar roof originally continued that of the hall but at a later date a higher new roof with east and west gables was provided at right angles to the original.

Under the hall and solar were dark unheated storage rooms entered by doorways on either side of the wall dividing them. The doorway to the hall undercroft has now been converted into a recess. This undercroft now contains several rooms and a passageway on the east side, where there is one original window and the head of another above the later doorway now forming the hostel main entrance. These windows have square heads, although their outer arches have pointed heads. The solar undercroft now contains the hostel toilets and washrooms.

Projecting from the hall-block east face is a two storey block 9.4m long by 6m wide over walls 0.8m thick which was built c1300 to replace a timber structure of the 1230s probably of similar size and purpose. The chapel lay on the upper level, with a lobby for a timber stair between it and the hall doorway. A trefoil-headed piscina remains in the SE corner and there is a three-light east window, originally with flowing tracery in the head. The plain mullioned side windows are modern.

The fine gatehouse of 1292-3 has similarities in its planning to several other gatehouses in Edward I's new castles in North Wales. It measures by 10.1m by 16m and has walls up to 2.1m thick pierced by many embrasures with inner arches that are almost flat, and rounded on their inner edges. On the north side twin round towers rising from polygonal bases with triangular spurs flank a passageway initially 3m wide. The passageway was closed by three portcullises, an outer one which had no groove in the lower part (a rather curious arrangement), an inner portcullis making the passage secure against the court, and a middle one just before a rebate for a pair of doors. The section of passage south of the middle portcullis is narrower and now open to the sky, since the chambers above this part are roofless. The vault of the outer part has been rebuilt and consequently lacks the normal murder holes for dropping missiles on intruders.

Flanking the entrance passage from north to south were polygonal rooms in the drum towers, then rectangular inner rooms, and finally passages to staircases in the southern corners. This explains the pairs of low doorways with portcullis grooves placed close together at the south end of the passage. The thin walls dividing the inner rooms from the staircase passages have been destroyed and not much remains of the staircases. What were once arrow-loops in the drum tower rooms covering the front of the middle portcullis have been later opened out as doorways, the portcullis groove being cut away as a result. The drum-tower rooms were reached from the inner rooms by passages, off which led latrines in the outer walls. The west latrine is now a cleaner's store cupboard and the east latrine now contains a staircase.

*Gateway passage at St Briavels*

*Hall window at St Briavels*

*The gatehouse at St Briavels*

The openings in the lowest stage of the gatehouse were once cross-loops with the arms ending in oillettes (roundels) and set in embrasures just wide enough to take an archer or crossbowman. Except for one loop on the west they have been replaced by windows as wide as the embrasures. The lowest drum-tower room on the west is called the Porter's Lodge, its probable original purpose. The east room is called the Oubliette Chamber since a hatch in its floor gives access to a dark circular pit prison. Over the SE corner of the building and the southern half of the entrance passageway lay the constable's hall with a fireplace and embrasures containing seats and two-light windows facing east and south. The SE stair continued up to a similar room above which formed the constable's bedroom. These southern upper rooms are roofless but the second and third storey rooms of the drum-towers remain in use as dormitories. The western inner room at second storey level forms a lobby containing timber stairs and toilets and retains an original two-light window with seats facing west. The toilets lie where there was once another spiral staircase leading upwards, since the stair from the lowest level in the SW corner terminated at this level. The upper part of this secondary stair survives higher up, where it leads out onto the roof. The original wall-walks and battlements had vanished by the 18th century when there was a roof overhanging the outer walls, as now, but higher pitched.

The excavations of the early 1970s revealed the footings of a secession of stone buildings on the east side of the court, where a late medieval fireplace survives in the east outer wall, and roof-mark remains on the north. These buildings are thought to have been used for forging and were demolished c1700, but they may originally have been domestic in purpose, possibly the knights' chamber mentioned in 13th century records. The fireplace replaces an earlier one and the hunting-horn chimney of c1300 on the solar gable originally stood on the wall-head here.

*The Dungeon Tower at Sudeley Castle*

## SOUDLEY RINGWORK   SO 661106   F

The point of a steep-sided promontory east of the church is cut off by a 45m long section of a 2.5m high rampart with a ditch in front.

## SOUTH CERNEY CASTLE   SU 047976

Of the recently erected castle captured by King Stephen in 1139 and recaptured by Robert of Gloucester in 1140 there remains only a length of the ditch. The site is flat and offers no natural advantage for defence.

## STOWE RINGWORK   SO 564064   V

This damaged ringwork 30m across and up to 3m high is a possible predecessor of the castle at St Briavels just 2km to the south.

## SUDELEY CASTLE    SP 032276    O

The castle captured for King Stephen by Waleran, Earl of Worcester in 1139 may have been on the present site, or on another site closer to Winchcombe. Milo of Gloucester failed to retake the castle in 1140 but later that year it fell to Robert of Gloucester. King Stephen himself captured the castle in 1144. The existing building was begun c1450 by Ralph Boteler, supposedly from the proceeds of ransoms obtained during the French wars. After it was forfeited in 1469 Sudeley was granted to Edward IV's youngest brother, Richard, Duke of Gloucester, who became king himself in 1483. He built the chambers on the east side of the inner court.

Henry VII granted the castle to his brother Jasper Tudor, Earl of Pembroke, on whose death it reverted to the Crown, thus remaining until 1547, when it was granted to Thomas, Lord Seymour, who later that year married Henry VIII's widow Katherine Parr. She was buried in the chapel beside the castle after dying following delivery of a short-lived daughter in 1548. Thomas Seymour was executed for treason shortly afterwards and Sudeley was then granted to Sir John Brydges, who was created Lord Chandos of Sudeley by Queen Mary in 1554. His son Edward, 2nd Lord Chandos rebuilt the ranges of the outer court. Charles I used the castle as a headquarters during the early stages of the Civil War. George, 6th Lord Chandos eventually changed sides, joining the Parliamentarians, to whom the castle was surrendered in June 1644. In 1649 it was ordered to be slighted and it remained in ruins until sold in 1837 to William and John Dent in 1837, for whom a restoration was begun. Further work was done in the 1930s for the Dent-Brocklehursts.

*Sudeley Castle*

*The east range at Sudeley Castle*

The castle consists of an inner court 47m by 37m externally, with on the north side, at a slight angle to it, an outer court of about the same size. Of the original mid 15th century building there remain the outer gatehouse, part of a tower at the NE corner of the inner ward, with a latrine projection beyond it, and the entire west wall 1m thick of the inner ward, with the 5m square Portmare Tower at the NW corner and the rather more impressive 10m square Dungeon Tower at the SW corner. This tower has a spiral stair in a turret at its NE corner and latrines in a projection at the NW corner. Its top levels, which contained fine apartments, are now open to the sky. The inner wall and most of the features of the west range between the two towers are of the 1850s, and an archway has been forced through the back of the former kitchen fireplace in a slight projection midway along the outer wall. The hall is assumed to have been in the south range, which is entirely destroyed.

The east range containing the private apartments was remodelled by Richard, Duke of Gloucester. It contained a splendid presence chamber in the middle over another fine room with a bay window facing the court. The upper room has a five-light bay window facing east and fan-vaulting and three other windows, one as tall as the bay and having two transoms. There were further private rooms adjoining the north and on the outside wall there is a polygonal staircase turret here. Originally there must have been an inner gatehouse in the north range. A corridor dated 1889 now lies on the site, although it contains two doorways dated 1614.

Except for the gatehouse, which has rooms on either side of the passageway, the outer court was rebuilt in the 1570s to provide lodgings at courtyard level, while the east range seems to have contained a long gallery accessible from the private apartments on the upper level. A fine fireplace downstairs is thought to have come from this gallery. The SW entrance into the outer court is dated 1887. The church of c1460, remodelled inside c1860 effectively forms a private chapel and lies closeby to the east. Some distance to the NW lies a huge ruined 15th century barn.

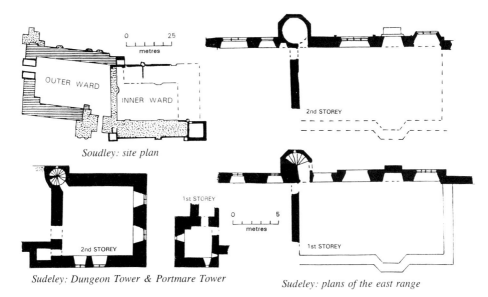

*Soudley: site plan*

*Sudeley: Dungeon Tower & Portmare Tower*

*Sudeley: plans of the east range*

## TAYNTON CASTLE    SO 747228    V

Earthworks at the above grid reference represent a low and worn-down motte with two baileys and outworks. This low-lying site was probably greatly strengthened by using water from the stream on the north site to fill moats. In Castle Wood on higher ground 3.5km to the SW at SO 715211 is a rather poor ringwork. The place name Mote Farm 1.5km east of this second site suggests a third moated or fortified site.

## TETBURY CASTLE    ST 890929

A bank near the church may be a remnant of a castle which was attacked by King Stephen in 1144. It was then probably fairly newly built. The bailey was captured but some of the garrison held out in a strong tower (probably of wood) until Robert, Earl of Gloucester arrived and forced Stephen to retire.

## TEWKESBURY CASTLE    SO 891321

A cemetery SW of the abbey lies on the site of a house of the earls of Gloucester. Here may have been the house which was destroyed in 1140 by Waleran, Earl of Worcester. King John's Pipe Rolls for 1211 mention bretaches or palisades being provided for this site. The house may have disappeared by 1471, since it is not mentioned as playing a part in the battle fought immediately to the south, when Edward IV (brother of Tewkesbury's then lord, George, Duke of Clarence) defeated Margaret of Anjou, her son Edward being killed, along with two of her principal supporters, the Beauforts. Margaret's name is perpetuated in a moated site at SO 896314, SE of the battlefield. There is also a damaged motte above a cliff on the east bank of the Severn on the Mythe (between A38 and A438) at SO 888340 (free access). Sir William Waller defeated a royalist garrison at Tewkesbury in 1643 but the Parliamentary garrison was later withdrawn to Gloucester and the defences partly dismantled. The town was occupied by Royalists in 1644 until a Parliamentary force arrived. It was again de-garrisoned and the defences slighted in 1646.

*Thornbury Castle*

# THORNBURY CASTLE    SO 634906    V

The Stafford family are thought to have had a residence on this site by the early 12th century. The existing building was begun by Edward Stafford, 3rd Duke of Buckingham, and was left incomplete after he was executed by Henry VIII in 1521 on a trumped-up treason charge since the king regarded him as a dangerous rival. The house remained empty until parts of it were roofed in 1720. Further work was carried out for Lord Henry Howard in 1811. His descendants remained in residence until the mid 20th century and further work was executed under Anthony Salvin in 1854.

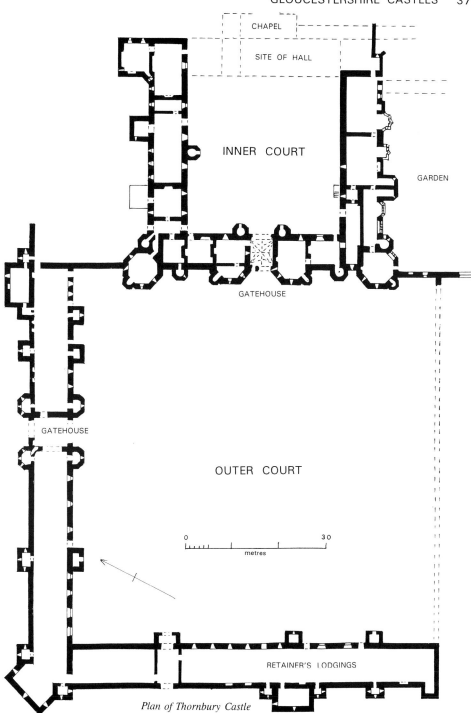

CHAPEL

SITE OF HALL

INNER COURT

GARDEN

GATEHOUSE

GATEHOUSE

OUTER COURT

0                         30
metres

RETAINER'S LODGINGS

*Plan of Thornbury Castle*

*Thornbury Castle*

The castle is best regarded as a stronghouse with four ranges around an inner court 33m square and two ranges of barrack rooms over stables on the west and north sides of the 80m square outer court to the west. The barrack rooms allowed for a large number of retainers, something specifically forbidden by the Statute of Livery and Maintenance of 1504. The castle was provided with portcullises to the inner and outer gateways, and with quite a number of gunloops, especially in the outer court, yet weak on the south side on the inner court, which was shielded from the churchyard by a high wall enclosing the duke's private garden. His apartments lay on this side of the inner court, this being the only part completed as intended, with bay windows of a curious design, including one which is cinquefoil above a lower stage with concave sides totally pierced with windows. The great chamber lay at the east end of the range, with the dining room in the middle. At the SW corner is a four storey octagonal tower 10m across, rising 16m to the top of the machicolated parapet and having a polygonal staircase turret on the east side and a smaller projection facing SW. There was a similar tower on the NW corner and between them lay the inner gate, dated 1511, and having a rib-vaulted passage flanked by towers of similar shape and size to those at the corners, with stair turrets facing the court. However, only the lowest storey of these parts was completed and nothing stands of the great hall in the east range with an apsidal chapel beyond it. Kitchens and service rooms lay north of the hall and guest rooms in a range projecting south along the east side of the privy garden. A gallery ran round the privy garden and from it was a private gallery leading to the church. Another court lay to the east. The ruinous outer court has polygonal turrets on both sides of the gatehouse on the north and there are closets in square turrets at intervals along the walls and on either side of rectangular towers projecting from the middle of the west side, the NE corner, and, set diagonally, at the NW corner.

*Retainers' lodgings at Thornbury Castle*

# UPPER SLAUGHTER MOTTE    SP 156233

On the south bank of the River Eye, immediately east of the church, is a small motte in which is a well. A small excavation in 1961 found pottery from the 11th century to the 13th century.

# WESTBURY COURT    SO 718138

The famous gardens administered by the National Trust SE of the church served a manor house of the de Mynors family which passed to the Baynhams in the 16th century and then in 1641 went to the Colchesters. During the siege of Gloucester in 1643 there was a Parliamentary force stationed in this house and in the detached tower of the parish church. The garrison later defected to the Royalists but were flushed out by Colonel Massey in May 1644. The house was rebuilt in the 1740s but demolished c1800. Old peoples' houses were built on the site in 1967.

# YATE COURT    ST 713860    V

A moat, now mostly dried up, surrounds a large oval area containing high fragments of a 16th century mansion, and a stone barn and a farmhouse with close-studded timber framing, both probably late medieval. There is said to have been a gatehouse with a portcullis groove and a licence to crenellate buildings here was granted by Edward I in 1299.

# A GLOSSARY OF TERMS

ASHLAR - Masonry of blocks with even faces and square edges. BAILEY - defensible court enclosed by a wall or a palisade and ditch. BARBICAN - Defensible court, passage or porch in front of an entrance. BUTTERY - A room where drink was stored. CORBEL - A projecting bracket to support other stonework or a timber beam. CURTAIN WALL - A high enclosing wall around a bailey. FOREBUILDING - A fortified porch containing the entrance to a keep and sometimes also the stairs leading up to it. A chapel was often provided above. JAMB - A side of a doorway, window or other opening. KEEP - A citadel or ultimate strongpoint. The term is not medieval and such towers were then called donjons from which word is derived the word dungeon, meaning a strongroom or prison. LIGHT - A compartment of a window LOOP - A small opening to admit light or air or for the discharge of missiles. MACHICOLATION - A slot for dropping or firing missiles at assailants. MOAT - A defensive ditch, water filled or dry. MOTTE - a steep sided flat-topped mound, partly or wholly man-made. MULLION - A vertical member dividing the lights of a window. PARAPET - A wall for protection at any sudden drop. PLINTH - The projecting base of a wall. PORTCULLIS - A wooden gate (sometimes sheathed in iron) made to rise an fall in vertical grooves, being hoisted up by means of a windlass. POSTERN - A back entrance or lesser gateway. RINGWORK - An embanked enclosure of more modest size than a bailey, generally of greater width but less elevated than a motte summit. SHELL KEEP - A small stone-walled court built upon a motte or ringwork. SOLAR - A private living room for the lord and his family. STRONGHOUSE - A mansion which was not fully equipped for a sustained defence against a proper siege but which would not be easy for malefactors to break into or burn down because of its solid walls and moat. WARD - A stone walled defensive enclosure.

# FURTHER READING

Norman Castles in Britain, Derek Renn, 1968
Castellarium Anglicanum, D. Cathcart King, 1983
St Briavels Castle 1066 to 1331, Paul Remfry, 1995.
A History of the King's Works, several vols, 1963-70
The Victoria Counties of Gloucestershire, Several vols.
Pamphlet guides are available for Berkeley, Sudeley and St Briavels
See also articles in Country Life, Fortress, Medieval Archaeology, and the annual transactions of the Bristol and Gloucestershire Archaeological Society.

*Sudeley Castle*